NO AR

# Careers For
# Wordsmiths

Interviews by Andrew Kaplan

Photographs by Edward Keating and Carrie Boretz

**CHOICES**
The Millbrook Press
Brookfield, Connecticut

Produced in association with Agincourt Press.

Photographs by Edward Keating, except: Lynn Chu (Carrie Boretz),
Kristin Landon (Paul Petersen), Pinkie Gordon Lane (John
Ballance), Susan Nover (Carrie Boretz), Julie Poll (Carrie
Boretz), Matthew Sweet (Carrie Boretz).

Cataloging-in-Publication Data

Kaplan, Andrew.
Careers for wordsmiths/interviews by Andrew Kaplan,
photographs by Edward Keating and Carrie Boretz.

64 p.; ill.: (Choices)
Bibliography: p.
Includes index.

Summary: Interviews with fourteen people who work in careers of
interest to young people who like creative writing.
1. Journalism.   2. Reporters and reporting.
3. Publishers and publishing.   4. Authorship.
I. Keating, Edward, ill.   II. Boretz, Carrie, ill.
III. Title.   IV. Series.
1991          070.4 KAP
ISBN 1-56294-024-4

# Contents

# Introduction

In this book, 14 people who work in language-related fields talk about their careers — what their work involves, how they got started, and what they like (and dislike) about it. They tell you things you should know before beginning a language-related career and show you how feeling comfortable with reading and writing can lead to many different types of jobs.

Many language-related jobs are found in publishing companies, such as those that produce books, magazines, and newspapers. But just as many can be found outside traditional media. Press secretaries use their language skills to help important politicians communicate with their constituencies, while lexicographers study how language changes and adapts to new social and historical circumstances. Songwriters and advertising copywriters demonstrate that the ability to use language in a catchy way can also be quite lucrative.

The 14 careers described here are just the beginning, so don't limit your sights. At the end of this book, you'll find short descriptions of a dozen more careers you may want to explore, as well as suggestions on how to get more information. Language is indispensable in the business world. If you're a wordsmith, you'll find a wide range of career choices open to you.

Joan B. Storey, M.B.A., M.S.W.
Series Career Consultant

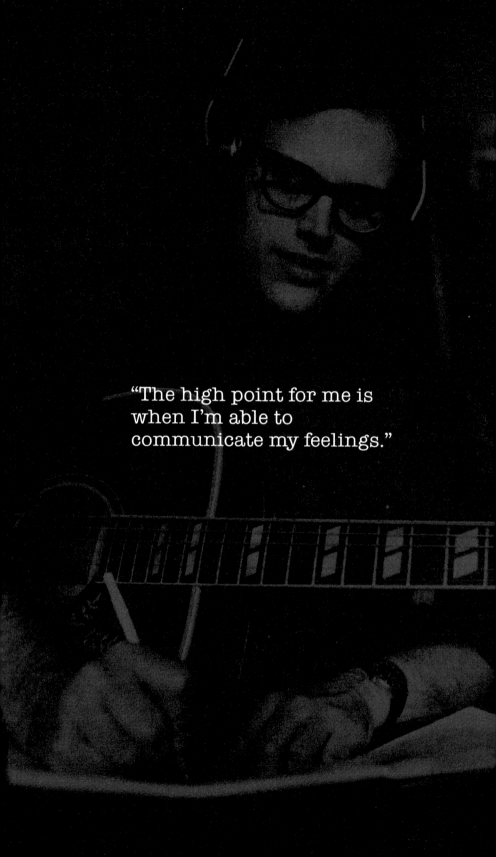

"The high point for me is when I'm able to communicate my feelings."

MATTHEW SWEET

# SONGWRITER

Princeton, New Jersey

**WHAT I DO:**
I'm a singer and a songwriter. I record albums of my own songs under my own name. But I also work with a music publishing company that sells my songs to other musicians. Some of these are songs I've already written, and some are songs that I develop specifically for other artists.

Songs are written in different ways. Some writers prefer to work with partners. One partner writes the music, while the other writes the lyrics. Sometimes I worked this way early in my career, when I was less secure about my ability to write lyrics. I composed the music, and someone else wrote the lyrics. But now I always write the music and the lyrics myself.

**Matthew works on the lyrics for a new song as he listens to a tape of the music track.**

Songwriting and performance are linked in different ways as well. Some songwriters don't perform any of their own material. They write songs that sound like current hits and sell them to other people. Other songwriters write only for themselves. And some, like me, do both.

**HOW I GOT STARTED:**
I have always been interested in words and in writing. Before I wrote songs, I thought about being a fiction writer. But the joy that I found in the music led me to songwriting instead. I think I knew all along that fiction writing would demand too much patience and isolation.

My involvement with music started in sixth or seventh grade, when playing the bass became my main thing. As I moved into high school, I began singing as I strummed my bass. At first, the lyrics were almost non-sensical. They were kind of like nursery rhymes, just words or phrases that had some sort of feeling to me. But I kept at it, and after high school I made a few independent records. At that point, some major labels began to show interest in me. So I decided it was time to become more conscious of what I was saying, and to be more open and honest in my lyrics.

My first music publishing deal was a result of my first record deal. People at the record company kept suggesting that I try writing with different people. They thought they could help me develop by pairing me with talented people. Now when people call my publisher, the opposite may be going on.

**HOW I FEEL ABOUT IT:**
Musically and lyrically, the high point for me is when I'm able to communicate my feelings. If the words and melody of a song can make me feel months later the way I felt when I wrote it, then I think I've done my job well.

For me, the hardest part of writing songs is having confidence in myself. Some days, I'll sit down and everything I write seems boring and terrible. On those kinds

**Matthew composes a new song on the guitar.**

**Matthew's job allows him to work wherever he likes.**

of days, I start thinking that nothing I've ever done was any good. Battling that kind of feeling and dealing with other people's criticisms are the most difficult things you do. But you have to keep taking pleasure in the process of your work, no matter what the outcome may be.

**WHAT YOU SHOULD KNOW:**
Behind a lot of today's big-name groups are stables of songwriters writing the hit songs. These songwriters are craftsmen. Many work in teams and have specific

strengths such as lyrics or melodies. Every few weeks, publishing companies send these people a list of groups who are looking for songs, or movies that are looking for title tracks.

The terms of a music publishing deal depend on the publisher's interest in the songs, its ability to get the songs recorded by successful bands, and whether the songwriter has sold songs before. Generally, though, you get an advance against the royalties the publisher expects you to earn from sales of your songs. The amount varies. For someone at my level, the range is $25,000 to $50,000 for an album's worth of songs. If your songs make more money, you get more money. If they make less, you still get to keep the advance, but your contract may not be renewed.

The most important thing is to have confidence, and to keep writing in the face of adversity. There are different ways for songwriters to break in. You can make independent records of your songs and get recognition from that. Or you can make tapes of your songs called "demos" and send them to bands, managers, and publishing companies. Basically, the idea is to get your songs heard by as many people as possible.

"I love the spiritual
satisfaction I get from
writing."

# PINKIE GORDON LANE
# POET
Baton Rouge, Louisiana

**WHAT I DO:**
I've published three volumes of poetry: *Wind Thoughts*, which was published in 1972; *The Mystic Female*, which was published in 1978 and nominated for a Pulitzer Prize; and *I Never Scream*, which was published in 1985. Almost all of the poems in these books were first published in journals and magazines, and then collected later. In addition to writing poetry, I also write reviews, edit poetry journals, give readings, and participate in poetry workshops.

Because I travel a lot, my schedule varies. But when I have the time, I'm almost always writing. I don't just sit around and wait for inspiration to hit. If I'm blocked, I sometimes use writing exercises to get going. For example, I might write about

*Besides writing her own poems, Pinkie edits poetry journals.*

an object on my desk such as a photograph. Or I might think about something I've read and that will trigger my imagination.

What I write isn't always successful. In fact, nine-tenths of what I do gets put in my "dead box." These are poems that I've had to mull over too much, and I know they won't be successful. But they're not really "dead" because I often go back to them later and find a few lines, a phrase, or an image that I can use in something else. And even when I don't salvage anything from them, that doesn't mean those poems were a total waste of time. At least they kept me writing and got my creative juices flowing.

**HOW I GOT STARTED:**
The year I graduated from high school, my father died. I had wanted to go to college, but I couldn't leave then.

11

**Pinkie reads one of her old poems for inspiration.**

Instead, I stayed with my mother and worked in a sewing factory.

Five years later, my mother died. I sold everything and went to college. I majored in English and minored in art. I was writing, but fiction rather than poetry.

After I graduated from college in 1949, I taught English in various public schools in Georgia and Florida. Then in 1955, I began working toward an M.A. in English at Atlanta University, which I completed in 1956. From 1957 to 1959, I taught English at Leland College. Then in 1959, I began teaching at the main campus of Southern University in Baton Rouge, Louisiana,

where I remained until 1986. At the same time, I was working toward a Ph.D. in English at Louisiana University. Eventually, I became the first black woman to receive a Ph.D. there.

In 1960, a poet I knew asked me if I ever wrote poetry. He said that he thought I had the sensitivity to do it. He also gave me a book by Gwendolyn Brooks, a black poet. She inspired me — so much so that it was almost a traumatic experience — and became a sort of a role model for me. I thought that if she could do it, I could do it too. That same year, I had my first poem published. I've been writing and publishing poems ever since.

**HOW I FEEL ABOUT IT:**
I love what I'm doing. I wouldn't change it for the world. I love the spiritual satisfaction that I get from writing. I love having it published, and I like the recognition I get from that. I also like the networking that's involved. I know a lot of poets, and practically every black poet in the country. There's a tremendous amount of interaction within this network.

A particularly satisfying moment for me came in 1989 when the governor appointed me the poet laureate, or official poet, of Louisiana. I became the first black poet laureate, and also the first poet laureate that a screening committee selected on merit alone. Before, poet laureates were usually politically influential people who happened to write poetry on the side.

**WHAT YOU SHOULD KNOW:**
Most poets have to support themselves by means other than poetry. A university is a good option because it keeps you in contact with young minds, writing, and language. But I've known poets who've done a wide variety of things to support themselves, such as working in restaurants or bookstores. One famous poet, Wallace Stevens, even worked for an insurance company.

To be a serious poet, you need to have a strong reading background in both classical and contemporary poetry. You also need to be concerned with the craft and the art of writing. You have to pay attention not only to what's said, but also to the way it's said. And on top of the reading and attention to style, you need to write as much as you can.

**Pinkie sometimes uses writing exercises when she is blocked.**

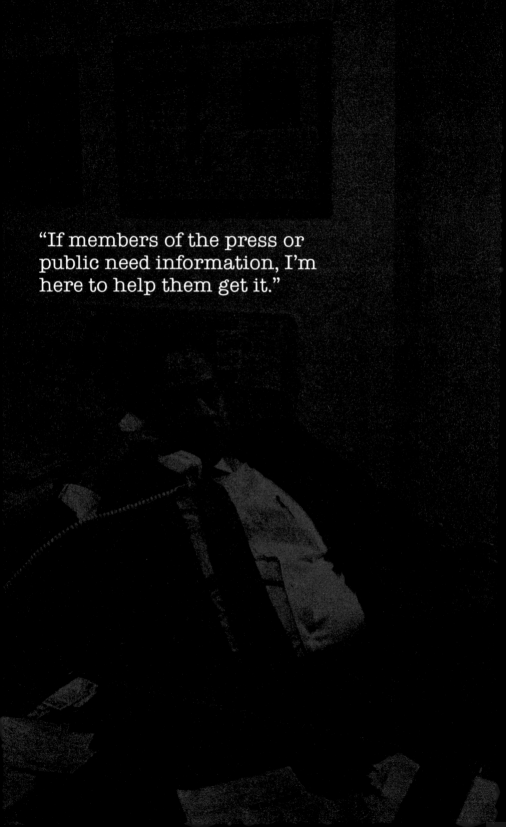

"If members of the press or public need information, I'm here to help them get it."

CLINT COLEMAN

# PRESS SECRETARY

Baltimore, Maryland

**WHAT I DO:**
As press secretary to Mayor Kurt Schmoke of Baltimore, I'm responsible for the flow of information between the city government and the press. If members of the press or the public need information, I'm here to help them get it. And when city hall needs to communicate something, it's my job to make sure that information gets out.

Holding press conferences is one way in which I provide information about city government. When the mayor is not available to speak, I speak for him and answer questions. But I answer questions at other times, too. When a reporter or members of the public need to know something about a specific subject, I'll talk to them myself or put them in touch with someone who is more knowledgeable, such as another member of the mayor's staff or a public information officer in a city agency.

When the government has something to communicate, I decide how this should be done. For example, there may be a change in an existing service such as the days of the week on which garbage is collected. To let people know about the change, I might write a press release and distribute it to the local media. If that doesn't get the information across, I might try other means — public service announcements on radio and television, getting a reporter to write about it, and so on.

**HOW I GOT STARTED:**
My first involvement with the media was in high school, where I was involved in stage production and the technical

*Clint answers a reporter's questions over the phone.*

15

**Clint talks to an officer outside City Hall.**

aspects of audio production. Later, when I went to college, I moved to the other side of the microphone. I got into newswriting for the radio station and did on-the-air radio reporting. I also began to see a career possibility that appealed to me. I thought that, as a news reporter, I could be an advocate for the public.

After college, I became a radio reporter here in Baltimore and for the next fourteen years worked in a number of news departments. I covered a variety of stories including local political campaigns. Two of these campaigns involved Kurt Schmoke, one when he was running for state's attorney and another when he was running for mayor. When Kurt Schmoke was elected mayor in 1987, he asked me to be his press secretary. Although he was familiar with my radio work, I've never really known why he asked me.

**HOW I FEEL ABOUT IT:**
What I like most about this work is the feeling that I have at the end of the day. I ask myself, "What did I do today to make a difference?" And more often than not, I can point to at least one thing that I did that helped somebody. For example, I may have gotten a phone call from a citizen who was about to be evicted from his apartment, and he may not have known that there were city pro-

grams to help him keep his apartment. Being able to connect him with one of these programs gives me a good feeling, a feeling that I didn't get nearly as often when I was a reporter. Although I tried to be a public advocate then, I couldn't see the effect that I might or might not have been having on people's lives.

**WHAT YOU SHOULD KNOW:**
There are not enough hours in the day to do this job. Often, I'm here at 7:30 in the morning for a cabinet meeting. And at 7:30 at night, I'm still here. I'm usually at home with my family on weekends, but I still spend some time writing press releases and taking phone calls.

There's no way to set out to be a press secretary. It just happens, usually to people in the press who have a wide range of political knowledge as well as public relations skills. The pay varies. Press secretaries for mayors in Maryland make from $50,000 to $65,000. Doing the same job for a governor, you might make more money. Also, in places with a high cost of living — such as Washington, D.C., or New York — the pay is generally higher.

In this line of work, it's your employer who sets the tone. I'm here because I believe in Kurt Schmoke — what he stands for, what he's trying to do. I don't think I would enjoy working for any other mayor as much.

**Clint attends a staff meeting with the mayor.**

"It's our job to protect the book."

# LYNN CHU

# LITERARY AGENT

New York, New York

**WHAT I DO:**

My husband Glen Hartley and I run a small literary agency. We find publishers for the authors we represent and negotiate the terms of their contracts. These contracts cover such arrangements as the advance payment; the royalty, which is the author's share of the book's sales; and the subsidiary rights, which include the right to publish excerpts from the book in a magazine and the right to turn the book into a movie.

We run our business out of our home. We get up each morning, go through the mail, and read manuscripts that have been sent to us. We also read newspapers and magazines to see what's going on and to get ideas for salable book topics. Usually we represent books that

Lynn reviews a contract for an author she represents.

authors produce from their own ideas, but sometimes we come up with book ideas and then find authors to write them. We're also on the phone a lot talking to authors and editors, checking on books already in progress.

After a book has been written and sold, Glen and I then do a lot of follow-up work. We help the publisher line up publicity for the book. We also check on the production schedule and, in general, serve as a liaison between the author and the publisher. A lot of the time that means explaining the publishing process to the author so that misunderstandings between the author and the publisher can be kept to a minimum.

It's also our job to protect the book. If the editor is fired, for instance, or moves to another publisher, we'll talk to the new editor and make sure that the book receives the attention it needs.

**Lynn's job requires a lot of telephone calls.**

**HOW I GOT STARTED:**
My husband and I have known each other since college, and we've always been interested in getting into publishing. After college, we both went to work for the University of Chicago Press. Then Glen got a job in publicity at Cornell University Press, so I moved with him to Ithaca, New York. At that time, I was thinking about going to law school and got a job as a paralegal.

After a year as a paralegal, I went back to Chicago for law school. In the meantime, Glen continued to work at Cornell University Press, where he was promoted to marketing director. When I finished law school, we both moved to New York. Glen became the associate publicity director at Simon and Schuster, and then associate publisher at Harper and Row.

During this time, I was working as an entertainment attorney.

After a few years at these jobs, we decided to start our own literary agency. We had saved the money we needed and also, through our work, had built up enough publishing contacts to make a go of it.

**HOW I FEEL ABOUT IT:**
One of the great things about having your own business is the freedom. We really do what we want here, and that's unbelievably different from a job in a large company where people are always telling you what to do. Also, because we only represent work that interests us — high-quality fiction and nonfiction — we get to use our taste and expertise on a daily basis in a field that we enjoy.

But working on your own isn't always easy or secure. You don't get a regular paycheck, for example. If you're not selling manuscripts, there's no money coming in. Also, because we're a small business, we do almost everything ourselves. There was even a time at the beginning when I strapped on a bicycle helmet and pretended to be a messenger so that I could deliver manuscripts to publishers myself. That was actually kind of fun. But some of the clerical and bookkeeping tasks aren't.

**WHAT YOU SHOULD KNOW:** In this work, it's almost meaningless to talk about pay and hours. They take on a life of their own. The pay depends on what you sell, and what you sell depends on what you can find. Right now, we have sixteen good books and we're pulling our hair out over scheduling them all. But there are also scary dead zones when the authors you represent are all in the midst of a project and you can't find a decent piece of writing to save your life.

If you want to be a literary agent, it's best to find work first with a literary agency, a publishing company, or a book store. There are a lot of things you need to know about publishing companies — how they work, what their needs are, and how the money flows — before you can work effectively with them.

**Lynn reads a manuscript that has been sent to her.**

"My job is to bring books into the public eye."

SUSAN NOVER

# BOOK
# PUBLICIST

Scotch Plains, New Jersey

**WHAT I DO:**

My job is to bring books into the public eye. I'm successful when I can get books and their authors mentioned in newspapers, in magazines, and on television and radio. I work for Grove Press, which publishes about 70 titles a year. I help arrange publicity tours for the authors of these books, and I also organize their book parties and bookstore appearances.

For some books, publicity is relatively simple. For example, if an author is already a celebrity, or the book is about a hot topic, you may not have to do much to attract attention to it. However, for most books, you've got to work. You've got to find an angle — a way to make the author, the subject, or both seem intriguing. Then you put together a press kit —

**Susan looks over an author's upcoming appearance schedule.**

pictures and written material — that sells your author and his or her book. You send out press kits all the time to television shows, radio shows, and publications that you're trying to interest in a particular book. Later, you follow up with more phone calls and letters.

Publicity work is different from most of what goes on in a publishing company in that it doesn't really begin until the book is published. Beginning with publication, however, we have a lot of author contact. We become the author's direct link to the publisher and to what's going on with the book. Authors call us all the time — sometimes three or four times a day — to find out what's happening with sales or why the book has not been reviewed more. We do a lot of hand-holding with authors, preparing them for their publicity tours and calming them down before television appearances. We try to be up-beat. We tell them they look okay, and afterward we tell them that they did well or give them hints on how to do better.

## HOW I GOT STARTED:

When I was a senior in college, a professor of mine knew that I was looking for a job. About a week before graduation, he told me that a friend of his who ran a publishing company was looking for an assistant. I was introduced to the friend, and two days later I went to work for her.

The company was very small. There were only four of us. As a result, I did a little of everything: I opened the office in the morning, took out the garbage, did the bookkeeping, and did all the public relations. It was a great, fast way to learn a lot about the business. However, after two years my boss decided to leave the company, and very soon after that I left, too.

My boss had always pushed me toward publicity because she thought that I had the right personality for it. She told me I should try to work at a large company, so I went to New American Library, a part of Penguin USA, to work in the publicity department. I wasn't happy

**Susan prepares a press kit to send to a television show.**

in such a corporate environment, and I wanted to work with books that were more suited to my taste, so after a year I came to Grove.

## HOW I FEEL ABOUT IT:

One of the reasons I like publicity is that, instead of editing somebody else's words, I do my own writing. We do our own press kits and our own pitch letters. We decide how to push the book, and in this way we're actually creating the publicity campaign.

Working with the authors is a mixed bag. I've met a lot of talented people, as well as celebrities, but it does have its drawbacks. For example, authors often work on books for years and years and they think about those books all the time. When the books finally come out, they wonder why everyone else isn't reviewing them and thinking about them all the time, too. They want to know why you're not doing more for them. They don't understand that there are a million other publicists and only a limited number of shows you can get them on. Authors also don't realize that their book is only one of the four or five books you're working on.

**WHAT YOU SHOULD KNOW:**
To enjoy publicity work, you need to be very social because the entire job involves deal-ing with people. You also have to be very positive, upbeat, and able to think on your feet. Of course, you also have to have a feeling for books and be able to express these feelings in your writing.

Starting pay for publicity work in publishing is low, only about $14,000 to $16,000 a year. But you can move up pretty quickly. Within five years, you might be making about $30,000.

The hours are basically 9:00 in the morning to 5:30 or 6:00 at night. But there are also a lot of after-work parties and meetings to attend, and you may also have to accompany authors on tour.

**Susan works on a press release for a new book.**

"I don't have a typical day."

DAVID ROSENBAUM

# MAGAZINE EDITOR

Boston, Massachusetts

**WHAT I DO:**

As the editor of *Boston* magazine, I manage a staff of twenty-three people, and together we produce a monthly magazine. I work personally with the copy, deciding which articles will go into the magazine and editing a good number of them. I also help create the look of the magazine. I come up with ideas for the art work – that is, the drawings and photos we'll use to illustrate each article – and I work with the art director on the layouts. In addition, my job includes organizational functions such as managing the budget and making all the hiring and firing decisions.

While I have final responsibility for the magazine's content, I don't do it all myself. There's the managing editor, who is responsible for the magazine's regular columns and works with me on feature stories. There's the lifestyle editor, who's responsible for the style section – the restaurant and wine reviews, and so on. And there's an articles editor who reviews query letters from freelance writers and edits the articles in the main section of the magazine. The articles editor also does some writing.

I don't have a typical day. One day I might spend editing stories. The next day I might talk on the phone with our lawyers or have a long meeting with the publisher about budgets and sales strategies. When I arrive at the office each morning, I usually don't know what I'm going to do that day.

**HOW I GOT STARTED:**

My father was an English teacher. Before I was in

**David assigns the articles and edits many himself.**

**David reviews the contents of next week's issue.**

kindergarten, he made flash cards for me with words on them, and he used them to teach me how to read. It was an intensive and effective teaching technique, and I learned to read at an early age. Since then, I've always been involved with words and with writing.

I thought I was going to be an English teacher. But after I taught at a college for a while, I began to realize that I didn't like academia that much. So one day, I wandered into the local weekly newspaper and said, "Why don't you give me a book to review?" I thought it would be easy, and a good way to earn some extra money. I was right in both respects. I also liked it, and I began writing more and more until I was offered the movie reviewer's job at the *Boston Herald American*.

I worked at the *Herald*

*American* for five years. Then I became the executive editor at a weekly called the *Real Paper* before returning to the *Herald American* as an editor. Three years later, I became managing editor here. Eventually, I was promoted to editor-in-chief.

**HOW I FEEL ABOUT IT:**
What I like best about this work is that I have a product at the end of each month. It's not something abstract. It's a magazine. You can look at it, pick it up, and feel it.

But the monthly cycle also has its drawbacks. A daily newspaper has a definite end. At the close of the day, you're done. But with a monthly magazine, sometimes it seems as though there's no definite beginning or end. At any one time, I might be working on three different issues – the one that's being finished, the following one that's being started, and a third one that's being planned.

**WHAT YOU SHOULD KNOW:** Most of the people I know who have done well in this work have started at fairly lowly jobs and worked their way up. You've got to learn by doing. And since this profession involves a lot of work, I'd say you need to either love the work or have no other options.

I didn't study journalism in college, so I'm not sure what it does besides give you contacts. But magazines now seem to be more interested in graduate degrees in journalism than they have been in the past. I'd say that a master's in journalism could help you get an entry-level position.

The hours and pay are long and low. You don't go into journalism, or any kind of writing, for the money. You go into it because you like it. There are some financial rewards. I make a decent living now. But I didn't for a long, long time. And I still put in the long hours, as do most people who succeed. Magazines tend to reward people who hang around. Some people may do their jobs well. But if they're out the door at five o'clock every day, they won't get promoted. Most magazines will promote the guy who sticks around until nine o'clock.

David discusses a story with one of his editors.

"I like being able to clarify who's doing what in the world."

RICHARD HYLTON
# REPORTER
New York, New York

**WHAT I DO:**
I report business news for the *New York Times*, and I specialize in real estate projects. I write about what's getting built, how it's being financed, and the story behind how it did or didn't get done.

Sometimes I work on long stories that take several days or several weeks to write. But more often I hand in a finished story at the end of each day. My days tend to follow a regular routine: Each morning I listen to messages from sources within the real estate field and return some of these calls. Then I talk to my editors about the stories they're expecting for that day. By noon, the editors give me an okay for a story, and I start writing. For the rest of that day, I make phone calls to get information, take a lot

Richard talks to a source about an article for the paper.

of notes, and write my story.

Towards the end of the afternoon, I write a summary of what an article is going to say and send it by computer to a file of summaries. Later, the editors look at all of the summaries and hold a meeting to decide which stories are going to be in the next day's newspaper and how much space each should get. After the editors make these decisions around 3:30 P.M., they tell me everything I need to know – the space that's available and any changes in the approach they want me to take. Then I have about two hours to write and file the final draft of the article.

Some of my story ideas come from the editors. But I generate more story ideas than they do. It's about a 60-40 split. That's because I'm on the beat, and the sources know me and call me. That way, I keep in close

**Richard listens to colleagues discuss a story.**

touch with the business circles I write about.

**HOW I GOT STARTED:**
I've always liked reading, and writing is just the other side of that. It's what produces the things you read. For me, it was a natural flow from one interest to the other.

Originally, I wanted to be a novelist, and writing a novel is something I still might do. But I found that journalism was a more practical way of keeping involved with writing. I got into journalism pretty early on, working on my high school newspaper. In college, I studied English, philosophy, and economics, but I also spent a lot of my time working on the daily newspaper there.

After college, I went to work for a book publisher, Macmillan, editing and translating for an encyclopedia of world religion. While I was at Macmillan, I also began doing some freelance writing for a magazine called *Black Enterprise*. After I left Macmillan I became an editor at *Black Enterprise*, and then a year and a half later, I became a freelancer again. Although I hadn't consciously decided to go into business writing, I found that there was a demand for it, and that I liked it. One of the clients for whom I did free-lance writing was the *New York Times*. Eventually, I was offered a position here.

## HOW I FEEL ABOUT IT:

I like writing, and seeing what I've written appear in the newspaper. But I also like being able to clarify things for people — to explain how things work, and who's doing what in the world. I also have the opportunity to travel, to learn about a lot of different things, and to meet different kinds of people. As a group, real estate developers tend to be very colorful, egotistical, and bombastic characters. So, I get to meet a lot of people who are very interesting and entertaining.

The most difficult part of this job is the deadline pressure. You have to work quickly and, at the same time, with accuracy. When you're dealing with daily deadlines for a week or two at a time, the experience can be very intense and draining.

## WHAT YOU SHOULD KNOW:

If you're interested in journalism, get a broad education. Study something else — English, economics, or science — rather than journalism. You can always learn journalism on the job. Also, try to work on school newspapers and, if possible, get internships with local newspapers.

To succeed at this job, you need to write with some ease and facility and to work well under pressure. You'd better like talking to people, too, because you spend a great deal of the day on the telephone. You also have to have a competitive drive. You need to be the kind of guy who wants to beat the other guys to the story.

The hours are pretty long — as long as it takes to get the information you need. The pay varies depending on the city and the paper. Reporters on large city newspapers, however, can make more than $50,000.

**Richard has only a few hours to gather all his information.**

"It's great to cover news that's important to my people."

# BARBARA GUTIERREZ
# CITY EDITOR
Miami, Florida

**WHAT I DO:**
I'm the city editor at *El Nuevo Herald*, which is the leading Spanish-language daily newspaper in the United States. We have a daily circulation of 97,000, which goes up to 125,000 on Sundays. Although *El Nuevo Herald* is distributed as a supplement to the *Miami Herald*, it's not a Spanish translation of that paper. Most of our stories are originally written in Spanish and are geared specifically to the Hispanic community.

As city editor, I'm a combination of a journalist and an administrator. On a typical day, I come in at 9:30 in the morning and review the list of stories for the next day's paper. Sometimes, because of things I've heard on the radio or read in that morning's paper, I add new ideas to the list.

**Barbara discusses the focus of an article with a reporter.**

As the day goes on, I talk to my seven reporters about how they should focus their stories and what the length of each should be. I also assign whatever pictures weren't assigned the night before. And I think ahead about what I'm going to do tomorrow and what I'm going to use for the Sunday paper. I'm always planning the Sunday paper because it has longer pieces that need more development.

In between these tasks, I do my administrative work. I help with the hiring and evaluation of reporters, answer letters, and perform community liaison work. I talk with community groups, speak to students, and in general try to keep track of the community and its needs.

**HOW I GOT STARTED:**
I've always loved reading literature and writing. In high school, I wrote and

**Barbara looks through another newspaper for story ideas.**

edited for the school newspaper. In college, I was torn between wanting to teach English literature, which was my major, and developing as a writer. After graduation, I decided to go into education. For three years I worked as an admissions officer at Barnard College, my alma mater. Then I went to graduate school and got a master's degree in journalism.

After journalism school, I went to work for *El Herald*, which was at that time only a Spanish transla-

tion of the English *Herald*. After five years there, I left the paper to work in television. But when *El Nuevo Herald* was launched as an independent Spanish newspaper, I came back to work on it. I thought it was an exciting experiment and that it would be a great challenge for me.

**HOW I FEEL ABOUT IT:**
There are a lot of things I enjoy about journalism. The work is varied, and you're often involved with interesting people and situations. However, I've realized that for me, the most important thing is covering Hispanic news. Because I'm a Cuban-American, I have a feel for this news. It's what I know best and like best. *El Nuevo Herald* covers Cuba and Nicaragua as though they were states next door, which is really thrilling for me. It's great to be able to gain expertise on these places and their issues, and to cover news that's important to my people.

The next most rewarding aspect of this work is the day-to-day interaction with reporters. They may come to you and not believe that there's a story in the idea you've given them. Or they may not know how to write it. But when you sit down with them, you can make them see the story and help them find how to write it.

**WHAT YOU SHOULD KNOW:** For this work, you should have a broad liberal arts background and get an undergraduate degree in something other than journalism. It can be helpful to develop a specific interest in an area such as business or economics, because an expert business or medical writer has a better shot at getting work.

Besides working toward a degree, you should work for the school newspaper and get an internship with the local paper. Even if you have to start by filing papers or writing obituaries, the training will prove invaluable. These days no major paper will hire you without three years of experience. However, if you're an intern somewhere, you may get a job through that.

The hours are pretty long. On a good night, I might get out of here at 7:30. On a bad one, I might be here until 11:00. But it's time spent in a good environment, in a small office with people I like. The pay depends on where you work and how long you've been there. In a small city, a city editor might make $30,000. On a major newspaper, city editors earn from $60,000 to $100,000.

**Barbara talks to a reporter out on assignment.**

"The pressure is part of what gives the work vitality."

JULIE POLL

# TELEVISION WRITER

New York, New York

**WHAT I DO:**

Over the years, I've had a lot of different jobs. For some I wrote, for some I did production work, and some were a combination of both. I've worked on a wide variety of television shows including soap operas, situation comedies, and a miniseries.

The requirements of television writing vary according to the kind of show you're on. Soap opera work, for instance, has its own unique structure. First, one or two head writers create a long-term story line. That is, they decide where the story will go in the next weeks and months. Then they outline exactly what each character will be doing: who's going to fight, who's going to have an affair, and so on.

Under the head writers are five writing teams, one for each day of the week.

**Julie works on the script for a new episode of a soap opera.**

Each team is composed of two writers: a breakdown writer, who scripts each scene, and a dialogue writer. The breakdown writers have to live in the same city as the head writers because they meet with the head writers on a regular basis. But the dialogue writers can live anywhere because all they need is the breakdown. They can have the breakdown mailed to them. Then they write the dialogue for the scenes it describes and send the dialogue back.

On the other end of the spectrum is a job I recently had as associate producer and writer for "The Shape of the World," a six-part miniseries about mapping. Basically, three of us put together the series — the producer, the director, and myself. There were two interview shows, two shows that I wrote, and two shows that the producer wrote. As

**Julie watches an episode she has written.**

associate producer, I researched, budgeted, and worked with the talent — the people who appeared on the shows and whose voices narrated them.

**HOW I GOT STARTED:**
I started out as an actress, but it's very difficult to make it doing that. Instead, I ended up as an assistant in the programming department at ABC. Because I had studied acting, and knew how to break down material into scenes, I got a job reading scripts and writing reports about them.

For a time, I left the business to have a family. Then, when I returned, the only way I could find to break back in was as a secretary. I worked for the producer of PBS's "Live From Lincoln Center." I was there for two years and got to do some

writing and research. After that, I wrote proposals for new shows for a while and then eventually got involved in soap operas.

The first job I was offered was assistant to a head writer on "As the World Turns." The job paid only $300 per week, and I had to do photocopying and secretarial work, but I also got to write the story notes that came out of the head writers' meetings. They said that if they liked my writing, they would train me to write soap operas. I took the opportunity, and that's what happened.

**HOW I FEEL ABOUT IT:**
It's a major high to see something that you've written on the air, and to know that millions of people are watching it. But on the way to that high there's also a lot of pressure. There's never

enough time to do things as well as you want to do them. And you can't miss a deadline because people are waiting for your script. One mistake can cost a lot of money.

The pressure can be difficult, but it's also part of what makes the work challenging and gives it vitality. What is more difficult is the unsteady nature of the work. You're almost always looking for your next job.

**WHAT YOU SHOULD KNOW:**
To write for television, you have to learn about what goes into the making of a show. And to learn that, you have to intern, stand at a copy machine, do anything

to get onto a show. It's the only way to learn about television's constraints — time, space, and sets — and how to write within them. It's also how you meet the people who can give you work.

The hours are very long, no matter what kind of television show you're doing. The pay ranges from terrible to fabulous. You could be a soap opera writer making $1,000 or $2,000 a week, or a head writer making $10,000 a week. On the other hand, as a freelancer, you may have to take a rate that's lower than you want just to get a prestigious credit, work on a show that interests you, or break into something new.

**Julie reads the long-term storyline for a series.**

"It's the unique combination of words and pictures that makes an ad special."

SAM POND

# ADVERTISING COPYWRITER

San Francisco, California

**WHAT I DO:**
I help create print, radio, and television ads for a wide variety of products and services. For the print and TV ads, I work with an art director, who's responsible for the visual aspects of the message. I'm responsible for the verbal message. It's the unique combination of these two elements — words and pictures — that makes an ad special, and more than just the sum of its parts.

The process that we go through is always the same. It doesn't matter what product or service we're advertising. The account executive, who's our client contact, brings us information about the thing we're advertising. We're told who buys it, what some people think about it, what the product does, and how it's different from other

**Sam works on the design for a television commercial.**

products in the same category. The art director and I then begin bouncing ideas off each other. I might have a line that gives my partner an idea for a visual. Or he might come up with a visual that gets the ball rolling. In a really good partnership, the lines between writer and art director begin to blur. Each partner has the primary responsibility for words or pictures, but both come up with visual and verbal ideas.

It normally takes a few weeks to come up with a campaign. Then we show our ideas to the creative director and the account executive's team. Usually, we have a few ideas. These might include a safe idea, which we know the client will like; an idea that we love but that has nothing to do with the account executive's strategy; and perhaps a mod or cool idea that capitalizes on some new trend or fad. Of course, you're never sure what will happen when the client sees your work. Sometimes you go in with a bunch of ideas and no one likes any of them. Other times, you only have one idea but you've hit the nail right on the head.

## HOW I GOT STARTED:

I started out as an actor. For six years I traveled around the country, doing a variety of acting jobs. After a while, though, I decided to change careers. I'd always liked writing, and I'd acted in a lot of commercials. So the job of advertising copywriter seemed like a natural choice.

By the time I got interested in advertising, I was 31 years old, and I didn't like the prospect of starting at the bottom. I wanted a job as a copywriter, not as an assis-tant, so I started to learn about advertising and put together a professional-looking portfolio. I talked to friends in the business and took college courses in con-ceptual advertising, portfolio development, and advertising strategies. Then I quit acting completely to work full time on my portfolio, and everything came together. About two years after I'd started, I finally got that copywriter's job.

## HOW I FEEL ABOUT IT:

The environment is great. You work with people from diverse backgrounds who are open, inquisitive, and lively. And what you're doing isn't like many other businesses. Your service is what's in your head — your ideas — and you get to apply them in many

**Sam makes a rough sketch for a new ad campaign.**

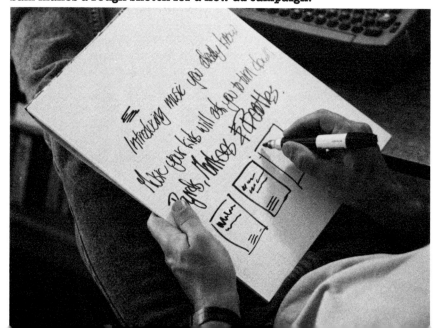

**Sam reviews one of the old commercials for his product.**

different ways. In the past few years, I've worked on ads for video games and beverages. Now I'm getting accounts for rental cars, a hotel, and a television station.

**WHAT YOU SHOULD KNOW:**

If you're just out of school, and you really want to be in advertising, there are a few routes you can take. You can work as a creative assistant, a production assistant, or a secretary to learn the business. But you're better off not going straight into this work. Advertising is one of the few fields in which it doesn't matter what you've done before. I've known writers who have done all sorts of

things. Your ideas are your credentials. Degrees don't mean anything here. No matter how old you are, you can always walk in and get an advertising job if you can convince someone that you've got what it takes.

The hours are quite variable, but no matter what level you're at, there's no time clock. You work until you're done, and no one looks over your shoulder. As for pay, you start off at about $20,000. A mid-level copywriter makes between $35,000 and $55,000, and senior writers make $75,000 and up. But you can also make a lot of money as a freelance copywriter. I've known some people who've made $1,000 a day doing this.

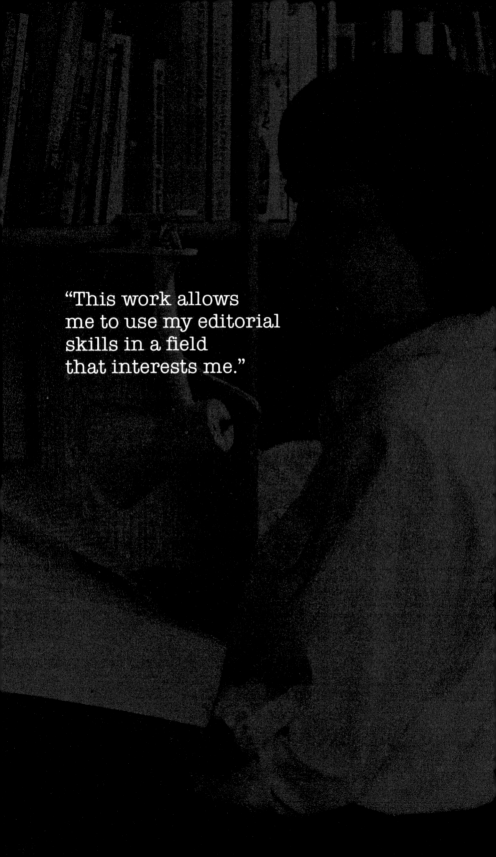

"This work allows
me to use my editorial
skills in a field
that interests me."

# KRISTIN LANDON
# SCIENCE WRITER

Eugene, Oregon

**WHAT I DO:**

I'm a technical writer and editor and I work on a free-lance basis, which means that I do different assignments for different people and publishers. As far as my writing goes, I've mostly done articles related to chemistry, which is what I studied in college.

As an editor, I generally work on high-level scientific volumes in the fields of physics, math, and chemistry that are used at universities and by working scientists. Although I don't understand everything at this level, I have enough background in physics and chemistry to follow the flow and see obvious mistakes. Catching those mistakes, in addition to clarifying the writing and fixing grammatical errors, is what I'm paid to do.

**Kristin fact checks all the technical data she uses.**

For my book assignments, I have a pretty set routine. I have four to eight weeks to edit them, and it's assumed that I'll work fifteen to twenty hours a week on them. When I get an assignment, the first thing I do is figure out how many days I have to finish it and how much I have to accomplish each day. That way, each time I go to work I know how far I need to get. I just sit down and plow through the number of pages I've set out for myself.

**HOW I GOT STARTED:**

I was always interested in both science and writing. As far back as elementary school, I was curious about the world and how things worked, and did a lot of reading about these topics. Later, in junior high and high school, my interests led me to science fiction and writers like Isaac Asimov and Arthur C. Clarke. I took as many

English classes as I could, wrote a lot, and participated in activities such as poetry workshops.

When I went to college, I chose chemistry over English. This was because, although I liked writing, I never thought of it as a way to earn a living. After I graduated, I worked for five or six years as a lab technician.

Surprisingly, the lab job led me back to writing. Because it was a small lab, we didn't have any clerical staff. The lab people helped the boss write up grant proposals and prepare research papers for publication. I enjoyed that work, and found that I was good at clarifying and editing things. When my husband and I moved, I decided to find an entry-level publishing job.

My first job was as a proofreader for a technical publishing company. After a little while, I got a job as a technical editor on a chemistry magazine there. Later, after three years at that job, I decided that I would rather work at home, so I made some connections and got some freelance work.

**HOW I FEEL ABOUT IT:**
This work is a good combination for me. It allows me to use my editorial skills in a field that interests me. When I was studying science, I

**Kristin edits advanced-level science books like this one.**

wasn't interested in it in a way that would make me a good scientist. I never had the bug that real scientists have, the bug to get in and find out something brand new all on your own. I just liked learning about science, keeping up with new developments, and stretching my knowledge. Now when I edit other people's work, that's exactly what I'm able to do.

This work might be more fun if I didn't feel so isolated. But there really isn't any way to keep the freedom I have and still work with other people around. Because I like being my own boss, and being in charge of my own time, I'm not willing to give that up just to work with other people.

**WHAT YOU SHOULD KNOW:**
If you're interested in technical writing and editing, the best thing to do is pursue the science side of it and get all the technical and scientific credentials you can. If you come in just as a writer, without a science degree, you'll probably be overwhelmed by all the unfamiliar material.

To break into this work, it's best to start out at a scientific publisher. Then once you have experience and a track record, people will be willing to give you work as a freelancer.

When you freelance, the usual way to get business is to send out resumes to publishers that produce the type of books in which you specialize. They may tell you that they don't use outside editors, or they'll get back to you and have you take a test, or they may offer to keep your resume on file. More often, though, you get work from people you've met during your years in the business.

Freelance editors get paid by the hour or by the book. The hourly rate ranges from $12 on up, while copyediting a book might earn me $400 to $1500, depending on how long and how technical it is.

**Kristin writes an article for a science journal.**

"The work is as challenging as the English language itself."

WARD GILMAN

# LEXICOGRAPHER

Springfield, Massachusetts

**WHAT I DO:**
I'm a senior editor at Merriam-Webster, which is a publishing company that specializes in dictionaries. While I've been here, we've put out many different types of dictionaries: elementary school, high school, college, and pocket dictionaries. We've also put out a handbook of English usage, a book of word histories, dictionaries of biographical and geographical names, medical dictionaries, and secretarial handbooks.

What I do depends on whether or not we have a major book in the works. Between major books, we do a lot of what we call upkeep. On dictionaries, this involves reviewing suggestions for revisions to our dictionary entries, correcting typographical errors, and making sure that we're up-to-date on

**Ward studies changes in the meaning and use of words.**

meanings and usage. Usage is the way in which a word is used. For instance, proper usage calls for *which* to be used to refer to things, *who* to be used to refer to people, and *that* to be used to refer to people or things. We're also constantly looking for and checking out new words.

No matter what major projects we're working on, we have a certain amount of dictionary upkeep to do every week. Later we will use this information to help us prepare new editions of existing dictionaries. For new editions, we check each entry against the examples of meaning and usage that we've accumulated since the last edition came out.

The last major book I worked on was *Webster's Dictionary of English Usage*. I was chief editor of that book, and I also wrote about half of it. The book was a historical treatment of English usage, in which we

**Ward works to ensure that the dictionaries are up-to-date.**

took the best-known usage controversies and examined them. One of my favorite topics was the history of *ain't*. I tried very hard to prove my theory that the word was of Irish origin. I found that *ain't* first appeared in the works of Irish authors of the seventeenth and eighteenth centuries. But when I found that an English author used the word *ain't* as well as Irish ones, my theory was kicked in the head.

**HOW I GOT STARTED:**
In high school and college, I wanted to be a writer. I was particularly interested in comedy and wrote a humor column for the college paper. I thought that I could step right out of college and write witty things for *The New Yorker* magazine for the rest of my life. Unfortunately, the closest I've ever come to that was a few nice rejection slips.

Instead, after college I was drafted into the army and then, when I got out, I went on to graduate school and got an M.A. in English. Jobs were hard to come by, however, and the first one I could get was in the second-hand book business. After that, I came here, not because I had a fascination with dictionaries but because I answered an ad in the paper. Still, it did turn out to be work that I liked and I've been here ever since.

**HOW I FEEL ABOUT IT:**
This work is as challenging as the English language itself. One of its most demanding aspects is responding to readers who send in inquiries about words or criticisms of dictionary entries. Many people bring up familiar issues about the usage or history of words. Every year, for instance, we get dozens of letters suggesting the origin of words such as *posh* and *kibosh* that we've listed as unknown. But some of these letters raise questions that no one has ever thought to ask before.

**WHAT YOU SHOULD KNOW:**
There is no undergraduate program in lexicography — the process of compiling dictionaries — as far as I know. Most of our people come to it as I did, starting out as editiorial assistants or proofreaders and working their way up. The hours are regular, from 8:00 A.M. to 4:30 P.M., while the salaries are roughly comparable to those of public school teachers, around $20,000 to $35,000.

To do this work, you have to like the quiet. We've had a number of people come to work here only to find that they couldn't stand the silence. The atmosphere is sort of like a library, with people flipping through books. When I came here, I was told a story about a monk who left his monastery to enter the real world. He started here on a Monday morning and quit by noon. As he left, he said, "This place is too much like the monastery."

**Ward reviews a definition in the card catalog.**

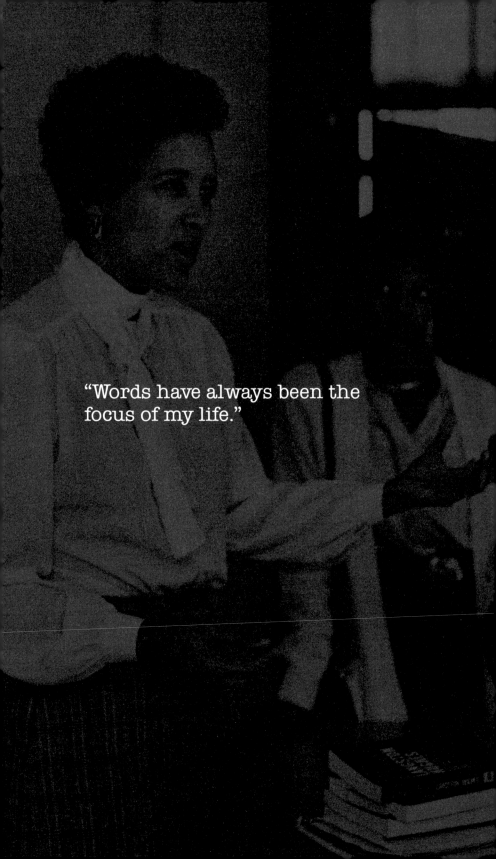

"Words have always been the focus of my life."

## AKIBA HARPER
# ENGLISH PROFESSOR
Atlanta, Georgia

**WHAT I DO:**

I'm a professor in the English Department at Spelman College. The courses that I teach change from year to year. Right now I'm teaching a course on composition, as well as a course on African-American literature. I also serve on various committees and am the academic adviser for forty-five English majors.

My schedule varies from day to day. This semester, my classes meet on Mondays, Wednesdays, and Fridays. On those days, besides teaching, I also prepare handouts, collect papers, return papers, and talk to students about problems with assignments they've handed in or are about to hand in. On Tuesdays and Thursdays, I write letters, articles, and book reviews, and I also grade papers.

**Akiba speaks to several students after one of her classes in composition.**

Another thing that I do on Tuesdays and Thursdays is go to committee meetings. I'm currently on the faculty agenda committee, which sets the agenda for monthly faculty meetings; the academic integrity committee, which works to promote honesty in the classroom; and the Founder's Day committee, which plans the annual celebration for the founding of the college.

In addition to teaching, writing, and committee work, I also advise students. Sometimes I help them with course choices, but at other times we discuss life choices. Students ask me things like, What do I do with a degree in English? Should I go to law school? Should I spend a semester abroad? These questions are hard to answer because you can't tell another person with certainty which choice is best. You can only help students think about

**Akiba teaches African-American literature.**

their options and consider what the results might be.

**HOW I GOT STARTED:**
Words have always been the focus of my life. I've always read a lot, and I've kept a journal since I was in the second grade. Later, in high school, I did some creative writing and worked with the literary magazine and the school newspaper. In college, I majored in English and read news on the campus radio station. One winter break, I worked at a radio station in my home town. I found that I hated it. So I got out of journalism and went into teaching instead.

My first job after college was teaching sixth grade. I didn't enjoy it because the students didn't want to be there and teaching every day was a grind. So I went back to my college — Oberlin — and became director of the African Heritage House, which was a dormitory that also conducted a program in African-American history and culture. As part of that work, I gave a course on the writer who was, and is, my greatest inspiration — Langston Hughes.

I also found out that college teaching was perfect for me. At that level, students bring more energy and interest to the classroom, the work is more sophisticated, and you don't teach every day. After I spent two years as dorm director, two of my former professors encouraged me to earn a Ph.D. degree so that I could teach college full-time. I got my master's and taught at three different colleges before completing my Ph.D.

## HOW I FEEL ABOUT IT:

The thing that excites me most is when I'm able to convince a student who has never read African-American literature before that there is real merit and beauty in it. For example, I had an honors student who had been planning to write her paper on Shakespeare. However, as a result of my African-American literature course, she decided to write about an African-American author instead. That type of thing is very exciting to me.

## WHAT YOU SHOULD KNOW:

If you're interested in teaching English, read as much as you can. Discover writers, read their work, and read books and articles about those writers. What led me into college teaching was that I enjoyed learning everything that I could about a particular subject, or a period in history. If this sort of intellectual pursuit appeals to you, perhaps you should try college teaching. But you also have to like researching and writing because part of your job as a college teacher is to do research and publish papers about your findings.

The amount of time that you spend on your work depends on your course load and on the demands of your research, but one of the great benefits of teaching at a college is that summers are free. The pay range is very wide – from less than $25,000 a year to over $100,000, depending on who you are and where you teach.

**Akiba discusses a term paper with one of her students.**

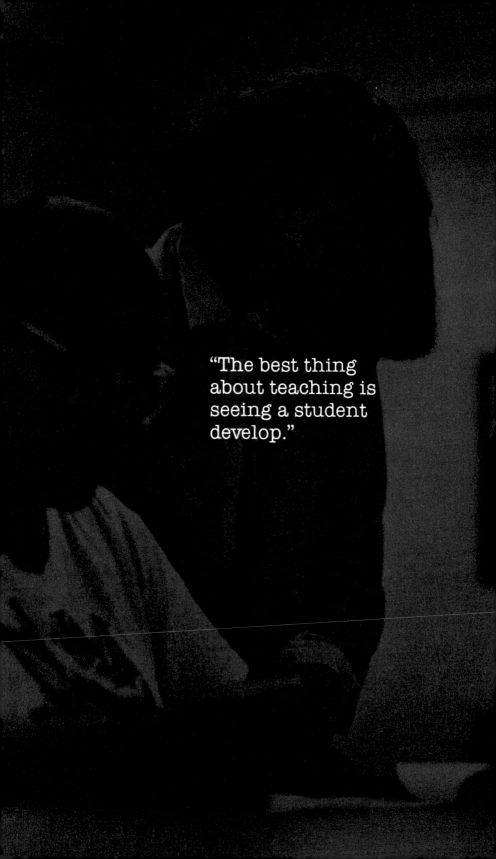

"The best thing
about teaching is
seeing a student
develop."

LYNDA ARGETSINGER

# ADULT EDUCATOR

Baltimore, Maryland

**WHAT I DO:**
I teach basic reading and writing at a center where adults receive remedial schooling, computer training, and counseling. Our program is designed to provide students with the academic and life skills necessary for them to become functioning members of society.

We have a mix of students. Seventy percent — most of them welfare mothers — come from Project Independence, which is a federal adult-education program. The other 30 percent come from the community and are people who have decided they need more education. Our stated goal is to help our students reach a ninth-grade reading level, and to encourage them to go on for a high-school diploma. But

these goals are really just part of an overall objective: to help our students function more effectively in society. We teach such practical skills as how to write a letter and how to read product labels.

**HOW I GOT STARTED:**
When I was growing up in the Philippines, we belonged to a church where missionaries taught Sunday school. I thought that one day I would be like them. I thought that I would go to the mountains in the Philippines and teach the primitive tribes who lived there how to read and write. I thought I would teach the alphabet to them — and at the same time, give them a chance to learn my faith.

I got involved in adult education in Germany, where my husband was stationed at an air force base. At this base, there were many infantry-men whose language skills were so poor that they were

**Lynda looks on while one of her students reads aloud.**

unable to understand weapons manuals. Because I had a background in English and reading, the base hired me to work in the adult education program there. After two years, I became certified as a reading teacher for adults.

## HOW I FEEL ABOUT IT:

The best thing about teaching is seeing a student develop. You watch the changes that go on and try to encourage that development. Beyond that, there's the pure joy of observing someone learn how to read.

## WHAT YOU SHOULD KNOW:

If you think you might be interested in this type of work, one way to start is as a volunteer. Many college students come in and tutor adults on a one-to-one basis. These volunteers also receive training from the permanent teaching staff.

To teach literacy skills, you need a background in reading and writing, as well as in psychology and the humanities. And you have to have a lot of love and patience, and be very accepting of people.

The pay in this program ranges from $20,000 to $26,000. School hours are 8:00 A.M. to 4:30 P.M., which includes one hour for preparation and one hour for lunch. In addition, because the instruction is individualized, you need to spend a lot of time at home, going over papers and preparing lessons.

**Lynda teaches reading and writing to adults.**

# Related Careers

Here are more language-related careers you may want to explore:

**BOOK REVIEWER**
Book reviewers read and evaluate new books for magazines and newspapers.

**BOOKSELLER**
Booksellers manage bookstores. They decide which books to order, how many to keep in stock, how to classify them, and how to promote them.

**CHILDREN'S BOOK WRITER**
Children's book writers specialize in children's literature, from textbooks to fairy tales.

**COMEDY WRITER**
Comedy writers write jokes, comedy sketches, and stand-up routines for professional comedians, as well as scripts for movies and television shows and articles for humor magazines.

**COPY EDITOR**
Copy editors read book manuscripts and magazine articles before they are published to correct errors in grammar and usage.

**CROSSWORD PUZZLE EDITOR**
Crossword puzzle editors review puzzles submitted for publication, evaluating them for accuracy and level of difficulty.

**DOCUMENTATION WRITER**
Documentation writers create the manuals that explain how computers and computer programs work so that non-professionals can understand how to use them.

**INDEXER**
Indexers compile indexes for books by deciding which entries to include and then examining the book to find the pages on which these subjects are covered.

**LIBRARIAN**
Librarians acquire books for libraries, manage their collections, and help members of the public find information there.

**LINGUIST**
Linguists study human speech and the structure and development of language.

**SCREENWRITER**
Screenwriters create screenplays for movies. They write not only the dialogue spoken by the characters but also the settings and the camera directions.

**SPEECHWRITER**
Speechwriters write speeches for politicians and other public figures to deliver.

# Organizations

Contact these organizations for information about the following careers:

**SONGWRITER**
American Society of Composers, Authors & Publishers
1 Lincoln Plaza, New York, NY 10023

**REPORTER**
American Society of Journalists and Authors
1501 Broadway, New York, NY 10036

**MAGAZINE EDITOR**
American Society of Magazine Editors
575 Lexington Avenue, New York, NY 10022

**TELEVISION WRITER**
American Women in Radio and Television
1321 Connecticut Avenue, N.W., Washington, DC 20036

**PUBLISHER**
Association of American Publishers
220 East 23rd Street, New York, NY 10010

**ADVERSTISING COPYWRITER**
Association of National Advertisers
144 East 44th Street, New York, NY 10017

**LEXICOGRAPHER**
Modern Language Association of America
10 Astor Place, New York, NY 10003

**TELEVISION WRITER**
National Association of Broadcasters
1771 N Street, N.W., Washington, DC 20036

**ENGLISH TEACHER**
National Council of Teachers of English
1111 Kenyon Road, Urbana, IL 61801

**CITY EDITOR**
The Newspaper Guild
8611 Second Avenue, Silver Spring, MD 20910

**POET**
Poets & Writers
72 Spring Street, New York, NY 10012

**PUBLICIST**
Public Relations Society of America
33 Irving Place, New York, NY 10003

# Books

**ADVERTISING MEDIA SOURCEBOOK AND WORKBOOK**
Second Edition
By Arnold M. Barban. New York: Grid Publishing, 1981.

**ASIDE FROM TEACHING, WHAT IN THE WORLD CAN YOU DO?**
**CAREER STRATEGIES FOR LIBERAL ARTS GRADUATES**
By Dorothy K. Bestor. Seattle: University of Washington Press, 1982.

**CAREER CHOICES FOR STUDENTS OF ENGLISH**
New York: Walker & Co., 1986.

**EXPLORING CAREERS IN BROADCAST JOURNALISM**
By Rod Vahl. New York: Rosen Publishing, 1983.

**HOW TO LAND A JOB IN JOURNALISM**
By Phil Swann and Ed Achorn. Whithall, Va.: Better Way Publications, 1988.

**JOBS FOR ENGLISH MAJORS AND OTHER SMART PEOPLE**
By John L. Munschauer. Princeton: N.J.: Peterson's Guides, 1982.

**LIFE AFTER SHAKESPEARE: CAREERS FOR LIBERAL**
**ARTS MAJORS**
By Manuel Flores-Esteves. New York: Penguin, 1985.

**MARKET GUIDE FOR YOUNG WRITERS**
By Kathy Henderson. Cincinnati: Writer's Digest Books, 1987.

**MASS COMMUNICATION**
By J. Bittner. Englewood Cliffs, N.J.: Prentice Hall, 1977.

**1991 WRITER'S MARKET**
Edited by Glenda Tennant Neff. Cincinnati: Writer's Digest Books, 1990.

**OPPORTUNITIES IN MAGAZINE PUBLISHING CAREERS**
By S. William Pattis. Lincolnwood, Ill.: VGM, 1986.

**OPPORTUNITIES IN WRITING CAREERS**
By E. Foote-Smith. Lincolnwood, Ill.: VGM, 1982.

**WINNING THE CAREER GAME**
By Patricia J. Sumner, Marian Lee Hendrickson, and David C. Borchard.
Dubuque, Ia.: Kendall/Hunt Publishing, 1983.

**WOMEN IN COMMUNICATIONS**
By Alice Fins. Lincolnwood, Ill.: VGM, 1979.

# Glossary Index